TRANSMATH®

Teacher Placement Guide

John Woodward
Mary Stroh

Cambium
LEARNING® Group
Voyager LEARNING

ISBN 13: 978-1-60697-067-6
ISBN: 1-60697-067-4

182086

Printed in the United States of America
Published and distributed by

Cambium | Voyager
LEARNING® | LEARNING
Group

17855 Dallas Parkway • Suite 400 • Dallas, Texas 75287 • 1-800-547-6747
www.voyagerlearning.com

Table of Contents

Overview

Administration and Scoring Procedures

Interpreting the Results

Using Test Scores for Placement Decisions

Student Placement Tests

Purpose

The TransMath placement test is a group-administered assessment that helps determine the appropriate instructional placement for students into one of three entry points into the program: *Developing Number Sense*, *Making Sense of Rational Numbers*, or *Understanding Algebraic Expressions*.

The placement test is intended for students who score below the fortieth percentile on group-administered standardized tests used by districts and states to monitor mathematics progress. Based on their test performance, students can begin the curriculum at one of three main entry points.

Placement Assessment Features

The TransMath placement test measures content knowledge of a cross section of mathematical skills students are expected to master at or before the middle school level, with a heavy emphasis on the numbers and operations strand. The number topics represent the main differentiation between the levels of the program. Items from the other strands, such as data analysis, geometry, and measurement, are included on the test but to a lesser degree.

There are three TransMath Placement Assessments:

- Developing Number Sense
- Making Sense of Rational Numbers
- Understanding Algebraic Expressions

Deciding Which Test to Use

The appropriate placement test should be used depending on the skill level of the student being tested. There are several measures that may be used to determine this. A matrix is often used to determine this. Elements of the matrix include (but are not limited to):

- Standardized or state test data
- Previous math courses and performance in those courses
- Teacher recommendation or Individual Education Plan (IEP) requirements

Entry Point 1

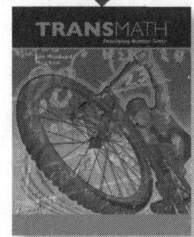

Developing Number Sense: For students demonstrating the need for foundational number sense skills

Entry Point 2

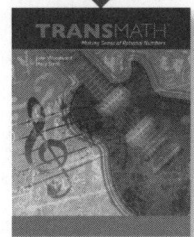

Making Sense of Rational Numbers: For students showing proficiency in basic number sense skills but lacking the foundational skills for rational numbers

Entry Point 3

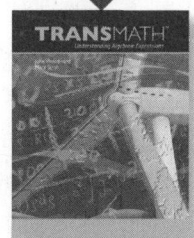

Understanding Algebraic Expressions: For students showing proficiency with rational numbers but lacking the foundational skills for prealgebra

Description

The TransMath placement tests were developed using traditional math concepts taught at or before the middle school level and guided by the National Council of Teachers of Mathematics standards and focal points. Items on the tests that represent concepts traditionally taught prior to middle school are included because they address commonly identified deficit areas found in struggling middle school math students.

Features of the TransMath Placement Test

Focuses on **number topics** that represent the foundational skills needed by all secondary math students, including:
- Whole-number concepts and operations
- Number theory concepts
- Rational number concepts and operations
- Prealgebra concepts and procedures

Provides a cross section of **secondary topics** that represent key mathematical ideas at the middle school level for the following strands:
- Geometry
- Measurement
- Data Analysis
- Statistics
- Probability

Consists of a **variety of problem types** commonly found on mathematics tests, including:
- Computation
- Multiple Choice
- Short Answer
- Circle the Best Answer
- Complete the Table
- Graphing

Integrates commonly used **mathematical vocabulary** and terms critical for understanding math concepts taught at the middle school level.

Yields a **raw score** and **percentage** that reflects a student's current knowledge of key math concepts to find the appropriate entry into the TransMath program.

Is group-administered and untimed and can be completed within one 50-minute class period.

This section explains how to administer and score the TransMath placement test. The discussion includes a) basic administration procedures, b) specific administration instructions, and c) scoring.

Basic Administration Procedures

The examiner can assure a reliable administration of the test by adhering to the following simple rules:

1. Comply with local school policies and state regulations regarding test administration, interpretation, and issues of confidentiality.

2. If a student has a 504 plan or an IEP that calls for accommodations in a testing situation, make sure to implement the appropriate accommodations.

3. Provide an environment conducive to test taking, including a quiet room, good lighting, and appropriate furniture and writing tools.

4. Promote test-taking readiness by encouraging students to be well-rested and motivated.

5. Review the specific directions for administration and scoring provided for the TransMath Placement Test prior to the testing session.

6. Deliver the instructions for the test verbatim.

7. Repeat the instructions as many times as needed.

8. No practicing of the test or studying of the topics on the test should take place either before or after the test is administered.

9. Do not use the test as a formative tool. Do not correct students' errors.

10. Allow about 50 minutes for students to complete the test. Take one class period for each test administration.

11. Keep the test in a secure place. Distribute the booklets immediately before testing, and collect them as soon as a testing session is done.

12. Encourage students to do their best.

This test can be administered to entire classes, to small groups, or to individual students (e.g., to a student receiving remedial instruction or to a special education student). The same basic instructions are used for all forms.

Specific Administration Instructions

The following administration instructions apply when administering the TransMath placement tests. There are instructions that apply to all three placement tests as well as specific instructions for unique items found on individual tests. To administer the placement test, each student needs two sharpened No. 2 pencils and one small blank sheet of scratch paper.

Step 1

Distribute one TransMath placement test to each student. Have students turn to the first page of the assessment:

> *Developing Number Sense*: Page 1

> *Making Sense of Rational Numbers*: Page 7

> *Understanding Algebraic Expressions*: Page 13

Hold up a test booklet to show students the correct page. Check that all students have opened their booklets to the correct page.

Step 2

When everyone has found the page:

Say:

> **Today you will take the TransMath placement test. Read the directions carefully for each part. You will be asked to answer different kinds of questions.**

> **In some parts of the test, you are asked to solve problems. You can use scratch paper if needed but be sure to write your answer on the test paper and not just on the scratch paper when you compute an answer.**

> **In other parts of the test, you are asked to answer multiple-choice questions. Read the questions and choices very carefully before making your selection. Once you decide on your answer, write the letter of your selection on the line following the question.**

> **In some parts of the test, you are asked to write a short answer. This might mean filling in numbers or words in a table or on a blank line.**

The following instructions are assessment specific. Read only the instruction(s) that apply to the placement assessment you are administering.

If you are administering the *Developing Number Sense* assessment,

Say:

> **In some parts of the test, you are asked to circle the correct answer. Read the problem carefully to determine if there is just one correct answer to be circled or if there might be more than one correct answer you need to circle.**

If you are administering the *Making Sense of Rational Numbers* assessment,

Say:

> **In one part of the test, you are asked to mark a location on a number line. Carefully make an X on the correct location. There should be just one X on the number line. Make the X dark enough to be identified clearly.**
>
> **In one part of the test, you are asked to place the decimal point in an answer. There should be just one decimal point in each answer. Make sure your decimal point is dark enough to be identified clearly.**

If you are administering the *Understanding Algebraic Expressions* assessment,

Say:

> **In one part of the test, you are asked to graph inequalities. Be sure to make it clear whether your circle is a solid circle or an open circle. Draw the circle dark enough to be identified clearly.**
>
> **In one part of the test, you are asked to fill in an *x/y* table. Be sure to write the corresponding *y* value for each *x* value in the table.**
>
> **In one part of the test, you are asked to draw a graph of a linear equation. Draw the graph dark enough on the grid to be identified clearly.**

Scoring the TransMath Placement Tests

Score the test using the answer key beginning on page 10. The raw score is the total number of items answered correctly. Compute the percentage by dividing the raw score into the total number of possible points, which is 35 for each test. The passing mark for each test is **80 percent**.

To assist you further in understanding student performance on the placement tests and to help identify specific deficit areas, the following breakdown of test items is provided for each of the three assessments.

Placement Assessment • *Developing Number Sense*

Content

This placement test is designed primarily to assess whole-number skills (operations and number theory). Material is also included to assess knowledge of the concept of fractions and addition/subtraction of fractions. The remaining material on the test comes from the secondary-strand geometry, measurement, data analysis, and statistics. The breakdown of items is as follows:

Part 1—Whole-number operations with multidigit numbers
- Addition, subtraction, multiplication, and division of whole numbers

Part 2—Number Sense
- The rounding of whole numbers and approximating of sums and products

Part 3—Number Theory
- Factors, greatest common factor, multiples, least common multiple, prime and composite numbers

Part 4—Fractions
- Concept of fair shares, equivalent fractions, and simplification of fractions
- Addition and subtraction of fractions

Part 5—Geometry and Measurement
- Symmetry, congruence, similarity, area, perimeter, geometric transformations, and metric units of measurement

Part 6—Data and Statistics
- Statistical landmarks, measures of central tendency, range, extremes in data, stem-and-leaf plots, bar graphs, and line plots

Percentages of Coverage for Placement Assessment 1

Whole-Number Skills (Operations, Number Sense, and Number Theory)
These items make up about **55 percent** of the test.

Concepts Involving Fractions
These items make up about **15 percent** of the test.

Secondary Topics
These items make up about **30 percent** of the test.

Placement Based on Student Performance
A score of **80 percent** is needed to pass the test. This means students pass Placement Assessment 1 if they are proficient in whole-number skills, and they have some general knowledge of fractions or other traditional secondary topics. **Students should be placed in *Developing Number Sense* if they score below 80 percent on Placement Assessment 1.**

Placement Assessment 2 • *Making Sense of Rational Numbers*

Content

This placement test is primarily designed to assess rational number skills (fractions, decimal numbers, and percents). Other number skills covered on the test are scientific notation and the concept of integers and addition/subtraction with integers. Material is also included to assess the secondary topics of geometry, measurement, data analysis, and probability. The breakdown of items is as follows:

Part 1—Rational Number Operations
- Addition, subtraction, multiplication, and division with rational numbers—fractions, mixed numbers, and decimals

Part 2—Number Sense (Equivalency)
- Equivalent forms of rational numbers—fractions, decimals, and percents

Part 3—Number Sense (Comparing and Ordering)
- The location of rational numbers on a number line

Part 4—Number Sense (Decimals)
- Determining the location of the decimal point in products and quotients involving decimal numbers

Part 5—Scientific Notation
- The conversion of scientific notation to standard notation
- The conversion of standard notation to scientific notation

Part 6—Concept of Integers
- The identification of opposites
- The ordering of negative integers

Part 7—Integer Operations
- Addition, subtraction, multiplication, and division of integers

Part 8—Data and Probability
- Tables, circle graphs, and bar graphs
- Likelihood of events—spinners and dice

Part 9—Geometry and Measurement
- Measurement topics of area and angles
- Geometry topics of types of angles, polygons, and geometric transformations on a coordinate grid

Percentages of Coverage for Placement Assessment 2

Rational number skills
These items make up about **55 percent** of the test.

Concepts Involving Integers
These items make up about **15 percent** of the test.

Secondary Topics
These items make up about **30 percent** of the test.

Placement Based on Student Performance

A score of **80%** is needed to pass the test. This means that students pass Placement Assessment 2 if they have strong rational numbers skills and they have some general knowledge of integers or other traditional secondary topics. **Students should be placed in *Making Sense of Rational Numbers* if they score below 80 percent on Placement Assessment 2 and above 80 percent on the Placement Assessment 1.**

Placement Assessment 3 • *Understanding Algebraic Expressions*

Content

This placement test is mainly designed to assess traditional prealgebra topics. Rational number skills are also included on the test because they are an integral part of students' success in algebra. Material is also included to assess the secondary topics of geometry, measurement, data analysis, and probability. The breakdown of items is as follows:

Part 1—Rational Number Operations
- Addition, subtraction, multiplication, and division with rational numbers—fractions, mixed numbers, and decimal numbers

Part 2—Variables and Translations
- The use of variables to generalize

Part 3—Inequalities
- The graphing of a number line
- Writing an inequality to match a graph on a number line

Part 4—Order of Operations
- The evaluation of numeric expressions using order of operations

Part 5—Properties
- Solving algebraic equations using commutative property, associative property, properties of equality, inverse properties (opposites and reciprocals), and identity properties

Part 6—Functions
- The completion of an x/y table of values for a function (symbolic to tabular)
- The graphing of a linear function (symbolic to graphic)
- The representation of a function using words (symbolic to verbal)

Part 7—Proportions, Rates, and Ratios
- The identification of proportional relationships in pattern cards
- The finding of the unit rate
- The understanding of part-to-part relationships represented by ratios

Part 8—Geometry and Measurement
- Properties of three-dimensional shapes and the measuring of volume and surface area
- Properties of angles, e.g., finding missing angle measures using the properties of vertical angles

- Properties of right angles, e.g., using the Pythagorean theorem to find a missing side and interpolating square roots when applying the Pythagorean theorem

Part 9—Data and Statistics
- The analysis of statistics in box-and-whisker plots
- The analysis of scatter plots
- The identification of types of relationships in data—direct relationships versus indirect relationships

Percentages of Coverage for Placement Assessment 3

Prealgebra skills
This material makes up approximately **60 percent** of the test.

Concepts Involving Rational Numbers
This material makes up about **20 percent** of the test.

Secondary Topics
These items make up about **20 percent** of the test.

Placement Based on Student Performance
A score of **80 percent** is needed to pass the test. Students pass this test if they have a solid foundation in prealgebra along with proficiency in rational number operations. These skills are considered essential prerequisites for entry into a beginning level algebra course. **Students should be placed in *Understanding Algebraic Expressions* if they score below 80 percent on Placement 3 and above 80 percent on Placement Assessment 2.**

Using Test Scores for Placement Decisions

Once the test is administered and scored, and the test information is recorded, teachers use decision criteria—in combination with other external assessment tools and teacher judgment based on student needs—for placing students at one of the three entry points in the curriculum.

In addition to the results of the placement tests, teacher judgment based on students' needs should contribute to the placement decisions. Standardized test results and other pertinent external assessments, portfolios of student work, and/or teacher recommendations can also be used to summarize students' learning needs.

Answer Key • Developing Number Sense

Placement Assessment • Developing Number Sense

Name _____ Date _____

Part 1

Solve.

| 1. | 43
 + 78
 121 | 2. | 71
 − 38
 33 | 3. | 207
 + 194
 401 | 4. | 307
 − 119
 188 |

| 5. | 39
 × 9
 351 | 6. | 52
 × 17
 884 | 7. | 634
 × 8
 5,072 | 8. | 337
 59
 + 1,508
 1,904 |

9. 6)46   **7 R4**   10. 9)738   **82**

Part 2

Round the numbers, then give an approximate answer.
Accept any reasonable rounding.

| 11. | 545 **550**
 + 322 **+ 325**
 875 | 12. | 598 **600**
 × 6 **× 6**
 3,600 |

Part 3

Answer the questions about factors and multiples.

13. What are the factors of 20?   **1, 2, 4, 5, 10, 20**

14. What is the greatest common factor (GCF) for 24 and 36?   **12**

15. List the first five multiples of 8.   **8, 16, 24, 32, 40**

16. What is the least common multiple (LCM) of 6 and 9?   **18**

17. Circle the prime numbers in the list.

(2) (3) 4 6 9 (11) 15 (17) (29) (31) 45 (47)

Student Placement Test   **1**

Placement Assessment • Developing Number Sense

Part 4

Answer the questions about fractions.

18. Which of the models is divided into fair shares?   **c**

(a) (b) (c) (d)

19. Add $\frac{2}{3} + \frac{1}{6}$.   **$\frac{5}{6}$**

20. Subtract $\frac{4}{9} - \frac{1}{6}$.   **$\frac{5}{18}$**

21. Write an equivalent fraction for $\frac{2}{3}$.   **$\frac{4}{6}$**   *Answers may vary. Sample answer.*

22. Simplify the fraction $\frac{6}{8}$.   **$\frac{3}{4}$**

Part 5

Answer the questions about geometry and measurement.

23. Which picture shows a line of symmetry drawn correctly?   **c**

(a) (b) (c)

24. The tangram shapes represent   **b** .

(a) similar shapes   (b) congruent shapes
(c) convex shapes   (d) quadrilaterals

2   Student Placement Test

Placement Assessment • Developing Number Sense

Name _____ Date _____

25. If the following two shapes have the same area, what explains the fact that the measurements are different?   **b**

Area = 16 units²   Area = 4 units²

(a) One is a square and one is a rectangle.
(b) The unit sizes are different.
(c) The sides are different lengths.

26. Find the area and perimeter of the rectangle.

5 in.
12 in.

Area   **60 inches²**   Perimeter   **34 inches**

27. Which of the following shows a slide (translation) of the triangle?   **c**

(a) (b) (c)

28. What metric unit of measurement would you use to measure the cover of your math book?   **b**

(a) meters
(b) centimeters
(c) kilometers

Student Placement Test   **3**

Placement Assessment • Developing Number Sense

Part 6

Answer the questions about data and statistics.

29. The median of the following set of data is   **21**

12 14 15 16 17 19 21 22 23 30 35 37 44

30. The range of a set of data is   **a** .
(a) the difference between the maximum and the minimum
(b) the difference between the median and the mean
(c) the sum of the maximum and the mode

31. Circle the outlier in the following set of data.

6 4 5 3 (50) 5 4 3 6 5 4 6

32. What is the maximum in the following stem-and-leaf plot?   **72**

3	2 3 3 4 5 6 7
4	1 1 1 1 2
5	2 3 4 5 5
6	1 2 2 2
7	1 2

33. The mean of the following set of data is   **b** .
1 3 4 8 9
(a) 4
(b) 5
(c) 6

4   Student Placement Test

Name _____ Date _____

34. How many more customers went to Burger Barn on Saturday than on Sunday? _____30_____

Burger Barn Customers Last Week

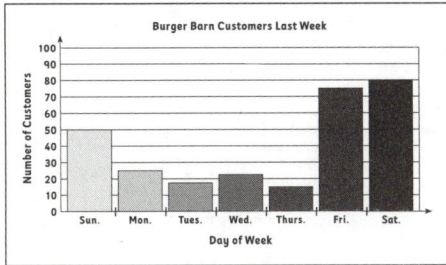

35. Between which two months did CD sales change the least?
_____April_____ and _____May_____

CD Sales

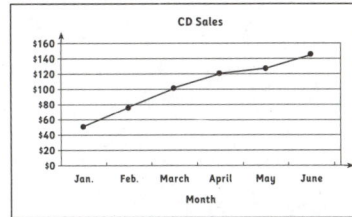

STOP

Page 7

Placement Assessment • Making Sense of Rational Numbers

Name _____ Date _____

Part 1

Solve.

1. $\frac{3}{4} + \frac{1}{2}$ ___$1\frac{1}{4}$___
2. $\frac{5}{4} - \frac{1}{6}$ ___$\frac{7}{18}$___
3. $\frac{7}{8} \cdot \frac{2}{3}$ ___$\frac{7}{12}$___

4. $\frac{3}{5} \div \frac{1}{5}$ ___3___
5. $9\frac{2}{3} - 7\frac{1}{3}$ ___$2\frac{1}{3}$___
6. $1\frac{1}{2} + 2\frac{3}{4}$ ___$4\frac{1}{4}$___

7. $22.7 + 39.18$ ___61.88___
8. $179.01 - 55.83$ ___123.18___

Part 2

Fill in the table with the equivalent fractions, decimal numbers, or percents in each row.

Problem Number	Fraction	Decimal Number	Percent
9.	$\frac{4}{5}$	0.8	80%
10.	$\frac{1}{4}$	0.25	25%
11.	$\frac{3}{4}$	0.75	75%
12.	$\frac{1}{100}$	0.01	1%

Part 3

Find the approximate location on the number line.

13. Put an X on the number line below to show the approximate location of 0.01.

14. Put an X on the number line below to show the approximate location of $\frac{2}{3}$.

15. Put an X on the number line below to show the approximate location of 30%.

Page 8

Placement Assessment • Making Sense of Rational Numbers

Part 4

Place the decimal point in the correct location in each answer.

16. Where should the decimal point be in this answer?
$2.2 \cdot 0.45 =$ 9 9 0 .990

17. Where should the decimal point be in this answer?
$44.2 \div 8.5 =$ 5 2 0 5.20

Part 5

Write the numbers using scientific notation.

18. Write 2.5×10^2 in standard form. ___250___

19. The number 3,700 is written in scientific notation as $3.7 \times$ ___10^3___.

Part 6

Answer the questions about positive and negative integers.

20. −5 and 5 are called ___b___.
   (a) reciprocals
   (b) opposites
   (c) irrational numbers

21. Which is greater, −9 or −10? ___−9___

Part 7

Solve.

22. $-2 + -3$ ___-5___
23. $-5 - -3$ ___-2___

24. $9 \cdot -4$ ___-36___
25. $-72 \div -9$ ___8___

Page 9

Placement Assessment • Making Sense of Rational Numbers

Name _____ Date _____

Part 8

Answer the questions about data and probability.

26. About what percent of her free time does Sarah practice piano? ___40%___

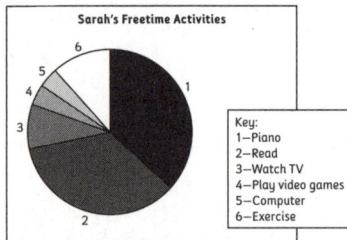

Sarah's Freetime Activities

Key:
1—Piano
2—Read
3—Watch TV
4—Play video games
5—Computer
6—Exercise

Page 10

Placement Assessment • Making Sense of Rational Numbers

27. Select the graph that best matches the data in the table. ___a___

Month	Sales
Jan.	$5,000
Feb.	$3,700
March	$4,600
April	$5,500
May	$6,000
June	$7,000

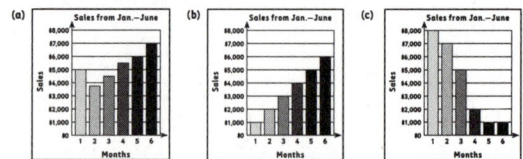

(a) Sales from Jan.–June
(b) Sales from Jan.–June
(c) Sales from Jan.–June

28. When you spin this spinner, you have the highest probability of landing on which number? ___2___

29. Which event is the most likely to happen when rolling two six-sided dice? ___b___
   (a) You will roll a total of 2.
   (b) You will roll a total of 7.
   (c) You will roll a total of 12.

Name _____ Date _____

Part 8

Answer the questions about geometry and measurement.

30. Which benchmark angle is closest to this angle? ___a___

    (a) 90°   (b) 45°   (c) 180°

31. The area of the rectangle ABCD below is 18 units².
    What is the area of triangle ABD? ___9___ units²

    A _____ B
    C _____ D

32. Which shape is not a quadrilateral? ___d___

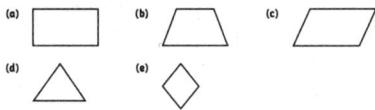

    (a)   (b)   (c)

    (d)   (e)

Name _____ Date _____

33. The following angle is what type of angle? ___a___

    (a) acute
    (b) obtuse
    (c) right

    Use the following graph to answer questions 34 and 35.

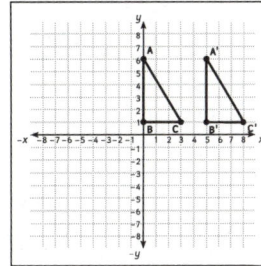

34. Which of the vertices of Triangle ABC has the coordinates (3, 1)? ___C___

35. What are the coordinates of the vertex C' on the translated
    triangle? ___(8, 1)___

STOP

Answer Key • Understanding Algebraic Expressions

Name _____ Date _____

Part 1

Solve.

1. $3.25 + 7.8$ __11.05__
2. $5.78 \cdot 5$ __28.9__
3. $\frac{2}{3} + \frac{5}{8}$ __$1\frac{7}{24}$__
4. $\frac{4}{9} - \frac{1}{3}$ __$\frac{1}{9}$__
5. $-17 - 59$ __-76__
6. $21.7 \div 0.7$ __31__
7. $-8 \cdot -9$ __72__
8. $-\frac{5}{6} \cdot -\frac{2}{3}$ __$\frac{5}{9}$__

Part 2

Select the general pattern that matches the group of specific cases.

9. $5 \cdot 0 = 0$
$-3 \cdot 0 = 0$
$\frac{1}{2} \cdot 0 = 0$
The general pattern is __b__.
(a) $m \cdot 0 = m$
(b) $m \cdot 0 = 0$
(c) $5 \cdot m = m$

10. $3 + 7 = 7 + 3$
$\frac{1}{5} + \frac{1}{2} = \frac{1}{2} + \frac{1}{5}$
$-5 + -7 = -7 + -5$
The general pattern is __a__.
(a) $c + d = d + c$
(b) $3 + d = d + 3$
(c) $-c + d = c + -d$

Part 3

Answer the questions about inequalities.

11. Show the inequality $x \geq 5$ on the number line.

12. Show the double inequality $2 < y < 9$ on the number line.

13. Write the equality shown on the number line using the variable w.
The inequality is __$w > 1$__.

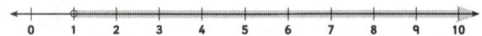

14. Write the equality shown on the number line using the variable z.
The inequality is __$z \leq 4$__.

Part 4

Solve using order of operations.

15. $3 + (2 - 1) - -2 \cdot 9$ __22__
16. $5 \cdot 3 + 7 - 8 \div 2$ __18__
17. $5^2 - (3 + -7) \cdot -2$ __17__

Part 5

Use properties to solve.

18. $3x + 7 + -2x = 10 + 2x - 9$ $x =$ __6__
19. $4(y + 2) = 3y + 7$ $y =$ __-1__

Name _____ Date _____

Part 6

Answer the questions about functions.

20. Complete the x/y table for the function $y = 2x + 1$.

x	y
−2	−3
−1	−1
0	1
1	3
2	5

21. Graph the function $y = 2x + 1$.

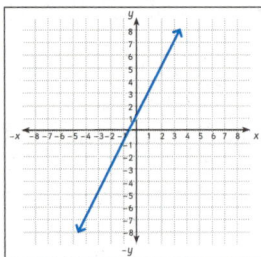

22. Tell the rule for the function. __$y = 2x$__

Input	Output
2	4
3	6
−2	−4
−1	−2

23. Which of the word problems is solved by $y = 3x$? __b__
(a) $m \cdot 0 = m$
(b) What is the population of my town if it is 3 times larger than your town?
(c) How many cookies did you sell if you sold 3 more boxes than anyone else?

Part 7

Answer the questions about proportions, rates, and ratios.

24. What two cards show a proportional relationship? __a and c__

25. Select the correct proportion and equation for solving this problem: If soup at the grocery store costs $4.00 for 8 cans, what is the price for just one can of soup? __a__
(a) $\frac{4}{8} = \frac{x}{1} \rightarrow 4 = 8x$ (b) $\frac{4}{8} = \frac{1}{x} \rightarrow 4x = 8$ (c) $\frac{1}{4} = \frac{8}{x} \rightarrow x = 32$

26. There are 17 girls in Mrs. Tobin's class. There are a total of 28 students in the class. What is the ratio of boys to girls? __11 : 17__

Part 7

Answer the questions about geometry and measurement.

27. Compute the volume of the cube. __64 square cm__

4 cm

Name _____ Date _____

28. In the diagram, what is the measure of angle a? _____45°_____

45°   135°
a

29. What number is closest to $\sqrt{37}$? __b__
(a) 35   (b) 6   (c) 3.7

30. Use the Pythagorean theorem to find the measure of side c. __5__

3
c
4

31. Rectangle ABCD has been reflected over the x-axis. What are the coordinates of the vertices of the image?
A' = (3, −5)   B' = (6, −5)
C' = (3, −1)   D' = (6, −1)

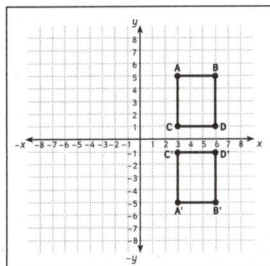

32. How many faces does a rectangular prism have? __6__

33. The surface area of a shape is __c__
(a) the length times the width
(b) the same as the volume
(c) the sum of the areas of the faces

Part 9
Answer the questions about data and statistics.

34. What is the minimum of the box-and-whisker plot? __68__
What is the maximum? __194__

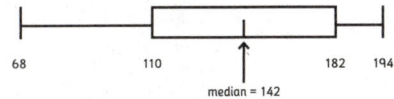

68   110   182   194
median = 142

35. The relationship shown in this graph is called an indirect relationship because __a__
(a) as one variable increases (driving speed), the other variable decreases (time to get there).
(b) as one variable increases (driving speed), the other variable stays the same (time to get there).
(c) as one variable decreases (driving speed), the other variable decreases (time to get there).

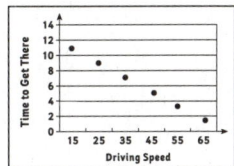